Robert Strand

Evergreen Press
P.O. Box 191540 • Mobile, AL 36619
800-367-8203

TABLE OF CONTENTS

INTRODUCTION

R. Gustav Niebuhr of the *Wall Street Journal* wrote not too long ago: "After a hiatus of maybe 300 years and much skepticism, angels are making a comeback." And, yes, they are!

It's not really a comeback because they have never been away. In our day of high technology there is also a desire for a high touch world. It seems that there are more people willing to tell their stories of personal encounters with these angelic beings. It's simply that there is more interest in angels today.

The Bible has always been with us and it's full of angelic visits to mankind and their ministries to us. To satisfy your own interest in the subject, I'd suggest that you get a good Bible concordance and look up every reference to angels. You will be surprised and reassured. Angels are another evidence of a God of love who is always watching over us.

This subject is much larger than can be covered in a little book like this. My hope is that you will develop a deeper appreciation for this phenomenon. Perhaps through these pages you will find a greater understanding of the mystery and excitement of an angelic encounter. And maybe after reading this you will look back over your own life and recall an event that had no plausible explanation for its happening other than that it might have been an angel at work in your life.

This book is a collection of angel stories, and to the best of my knowledge they are all true, factual, personal, real-life stories from the life experiences of real-life people. They have not been researched beyond the accounts of the people who experienced them and recorded them for us. Take them at face value as they have been presented. I believe that angels exist! My hope is that you, too, also believe in their existence. In most cases, the stories are based on written accounts or interviews with real people with real addresses. Their actual names are used except where they have asked not to be identified.

After you have read this book and enjoyed it, please pass it along.

Robert J. Strand
Springfield, Missouri
2003

DEDICATION

This book is dedicated to all the wonderful people who have so willingly shared their angel stories in the hope that they will bless and encourage others! Thanks for your help.

"An angel is a spiritual creature
created by God without a body for the service
of Christendom and of the Church."
—*Martin Luther*

Chapter 1

ABOUT ANGELS

Evangelist Billy Graham wrote that just before his maternal grandmother died, she sat up in her bed and said, "I see Jesus. I see Ben (her deceased husband), and I see angels!"

The editor of a well-known and widely read Christian publication reports that after angels were seen hovering over the hospital bed of his little comatose daughter, she awoke and experienced a full recovery!

The late Corrie ten Boom wrote that after her arrival at the Nazi concentration camp, Ravensbruck, she was hoping not to be searched because she had hidden a Bible under her dress. While waiting in line with all the other prisoners, she prayed: "Lord, cause now Thine angels to surround me, for the guards must not see me." She passed somehow, miraculously, through two sets of searchers without detection.

Is an angel "encounter" the real thing? What do we really know about angels and their ministry? Everybody

1

has some ideas about angels. Today you can find entire boutiques devoted to angels.

Billy Graham, in his popular book on angels, wrote: "Angels have a much more important place in the Bible than the devil and his demons." The Bible is full of dramatic angelic appearances to such people as Abraham, Jacob, Moses, Joshua, Gideon, David, Elijah, Zechariah, Joseph, Mary, Peter, and Jesus who, along with many others, saw angels and even talked with some of them. They are depicted in many roles: comforting people, relaying necessary information, climbing ladders, wrestling with people, taming lions, lifting great weights, announcing important births, and recruiting leaders. Angels performed such roles as warriors in battle and executioners, and they assisted in miraculous escapes and much more.

There are only two angels mentioned by name in the Scriptures: Michael and Gabriel. Michael is depicted in three books as the "Great Prince" or the archangel, while Gabriel is seen as presiding over paradise. Yes, I know, there is another angel mentioned: Lucifer, who is a fallen angel, also known as the devil.

Well, what are angels? A careful biblical study reveals the fact that they are created beings, dignified, majestic, personal beings with high intelligence. They represent God but are not omnipresent as He is. Little is said of their physical appearances, but it seems as though they can take on the physical form of a person and can even be mistaken for another human being. The word "angel" itself simply means "messenger."

In the life of Jesus, angels protected Him as a baby, strengthened Him in the hours of temptation, and ministered to Him in the Garden of Gethsemane. Thousands of them were available to Jesus while He was hanging on the cross, some angels rolled the stone away from the garden tomb, and two angels announced His resurrection!

Angels both announced Jesus' birth and told us about His second coming. They will gather God's children when the time of judgment comes. They will be a great host encircling the throne of Jesus and singing the song of triumph.

Our understanding needs to be opened so that we can ask God to help us develop a healthy balance in regard to His angels and their ministry. There is one thing which we must note: at no time should an angel be worshiped. That was Lucifer's downfall—he wanted to be like God, but the Bible is very clear that it is God alone who is to be worshiped. We are free to ask God for help in an emergency and pray that He will send His angels to give us assistance.

None of us has any idea how many times an angel has stepped into our lives to protect us! We may never know until we reach heaven.

For by him all things were created: things in heaven and on earth, visible and invisible, whether thrones or powers or rulers or authorities; all things were created by him and for him (Colossians 1:16).

FOOD FOR THOUGHT: One day, I believe, when we get to heaven and have the opportunity to look back on our days on this earth, we will be amazed at how many times God sent His angels to deliver and protect us from danger. Most of us will likely never see an angel in person but we are able to see and experience the results of their care and protection of us while on earth.

"One should not stand at the foot of
a sick person's bed, because that place is
reserved for the guardian angel."
—*Jewish folk saying*

Chapter 2

ANGELS ON VIGIL

The next several chapters contain accounts from people, with whom I have personally had contact, who desire to share their encounters with angels.

From *Misty Isaacs, Kingsport, Tennessee:* This story concerns my mother, Velma Ezell, her identical twin sister, Melba McCroskey, and Melba's daughter, Cindy Stafford. Shortly after Cindy married, her mother was diagnosed with "amyotrophic lateral sclerosis" (ALS or Lou Gehrig's disease), which attacks and destroys muscles and nerves although the mind is not affected. Her disease progressed rapidly and she was soon confined to a wheelchair and attached to an oxygen machine. She lived in this state for three years and never complained, but often spent her time in prayer for her lost friends and family. She had a sharp mind and a wonderful, uplifting attitude.

Soon she only had the use of her eyes, but could those eyes ever talk! A communication method was worked out so she could spell words with her eyes in which she would close her eyes for "no" and raise her eyebrows for "yes." When she needed to emphasize, she managed to utter a groan along with her eye motions. The system worked well because my mother, her twin, was really able to anticipate what was in her sister's mind because they had the unique connection that twins often do.

My mother, Velma, and Cindy took turns keeping vigil by Melba's bedside. We all knew the end was nearing when the family was called one day. Velma was alone in the room with Melba as the doctor broke the news. Velma closed her eyes and began to cry and pray while holding Melba's hand. Suddenly she felt a substantial hand placed on her shoulder, obviously for comfort. Her assumption was that it was the hand of the doctor, but when she opened her eyes to acknowledge him, she saw that he was not in the room. She felt chills and turned back to her sister whose eyes were wide open.

Velma told the sick woman about the hand and asked Melba if it was the doctor. Melba closed her eyes for "no!"

Then Velma asked, "Was it an angel?" Melba emphatically raised her eyebrows and let out a groan. She flashed her eyes around the room.

Velma asked if they were with her all the time, and she answered with an emphatic "yes!" Then she communicated that she saw them every day around her bed!

She didn't die that night, but lived a little over a month longer until the first day of spring. It was just long enough for her daughter, Cindy, to have her own personal angelic visit. Cindy was in the kitchen and was passing Melba's room to go the den. (Melba lived out her illness at home, and all these visits took place in her bedroom.) From the corner of her eye she saw someone standing at the foot of her mother's bed. She passed by again but did not see the figure. Cindy then told her mother that she had seen someone at the foot of her bed and Melba acknowledged with the familiar eyebrow and groan, "yes!" Cindy questioned the sick woman further, asking her if this was an angel and she received another emphatic "yes." She again flashed those eyes around the room to let Cindy know that her room was full of them day and night.

Visitors and other family members didn't see any of the angels mentioned above, but they all had the sense of being in the presence of something or someone very holy and awesome. What a source of encouragement to know that in this time of need the angels stood vigil until it was time to take Melba to her heavenly home.

After the Lord Jesus had spoken to them, he was taken up into heaven and he sat at the right hand of God (Mark 16:19).

While he was blessing them, he left them and was taken up into heaven (Luke 24:51).

FOOD FOR THOUGHT: Angels were present to give comfort when Melba's physical body let her down. They offered strength when her body had forsaken her. They provided peace and consolation to those who loved her. This was a glimpse of the tender side of God who sent a host of angels to cradle His child until it was time for her to be with Him.

"Angels are the dispensers and administrators
of divine beneficence toward us; they regard our
safety, undertake our defense, direct our ways,
and exercise a constant solicitude
that no evil befall us."
—*John Calvin*

Chapter 3

THE SNOWPLOW ANGEL

During the winter of 1987, John and Roberta (names changed) were in a crisis! Their four-year-old son, Benjamin, became deathly sick. What had started out as a cold had turned into the flu and eventually became a severe case of full blown pneumonia. His fever elevated to 104°, and he became delirious, drifting in and out of consciousness. The nearest hospital was more than 30 miles from the family's Colorado ranch near Glenwood Springs. That's not too far when road conditions are good, but when your child needs immediate help and there is a raging western snowstorm outside, it's like a thousand miles

13

away. The doctor advised them to get Benjamin to the hospital as quickly as possible, if it was possible at all since all roads in and out of Glenwood Springs were blocked with snow and drifts.

John prepared his truck, a four-wheel-drive Ford F-350 with chains, extra blankets, lots of hot coffee, road flares, a shovel, some food, and emergency candles. Even with these provisions, however, it would be a tough trip. He backed out of the shed and slid to a stop by the side door where Roberta was anxiously waiting with Benjamin all bundled up to protect him from the bitter cold. Before they started on their perilous journey to the hospital, John prayed a simple, desperate prayer for help: "Lord, you see our need. Benjamin is sick and could die. Watch over us and protect us on our mission of mercy. Amen."

Along the way, they encountered drifts as high as six or seven feet and had to break right through them on the two miles of gravel road that led to the highway. Their hopes soared when they discovered the main road had recently been plowed and they would be able to cover the next 15 miles with no trouble. But then the road conditions abruptly changed for the worse. As they looked to the right, their hearts fell as they saw the snowplow, broken down and buried in drifting snow. The road ahead was covered everywhere with at least three feet of snow and drifts of six or seven feet. They had little choice, so they continued on. It was slow going, but they were able to keep going.

Suddenly, Eric shouted, "Oh, no!" The truck tilted hard to the right and dropped into a hole! A part of the highway had collapsed, leaving a four foot gaping hole into which the truck's front end had dropped with the frame resting on the edge of the pavement! It looked as if their journey was finished. They were stuck and Glenwood Springs was still seven miles away! Eric prayed again: "Lord, I've not asked for much. Can You help us now? Amen!"

Soon, they heard the sounds of a heavy diesel engine behind them—it was the broken down snowplow at work once again! John told Roberta everything would be okay and ran back to meet the plow. A young man was driving and had a huge smile for John as he asked, "Can you help us?"

The man replied, "That's why I'm here." A chain was quickly attached to the Ford pickup, and the truck was pulled out. There was no serious damage to the under-carriage, so the young man said, "Follow me. I'll plow the road for you." In what seemed like no time at all, they reached the city limits and pulled into the hospital parking lot. When they got Benjamin safely inside, the doctors said they had arrived just in time. Had they been delayed any longer, he might not have survived. Benjamin recovered, and John gave the credit to the snowplow driver.

To show his appreciation, John called the county maintenance office and asked for the supervisor. When he came on the line, John told him what had happened and asked for the driver's name because they owed him so much and wanted to personally express their appreciation.

There was a long pause on the line and the supervisor finally said: "Well, sir, the snowplow you're talking about is driven by Lonnie Mickes, but he's not here. His truck busted a transmission yesterday about seven miles out of town. It's still sitting out there, so Lonnie went home. He won't be back in until tomorrow morning when we hope to have another rig ready for him to use."

Praise the LORD, you his angels, you mighty ones who do his bidding, who obey his word. Praise the LORD, all his heavenly hosts, you his servants who do his will. Praise the LORD, all his works everywhere in his dominion. Praise the LORD, O my soul (Psalm 103:20-22).

FOOD FOR THOUGHT: Angels can get so absorbed in their work that their appearance is dictated by their special assignment. Depending upon their assigned task in serving us, they may remain invisible or appear in ordinary human form. Their form depends on their function in the mission they have been sent on to accomplish. J. M. Wilson wrote: "In general they are simply regarded as embodiments of their mission."

"We may not be aware of the presence
of angels. We can't always predict how they
will appear. But angels have been said to be our
neighbors. Often they may be our
companions without our being
aware of their presence."
—*Billy Graham*

Chapter 4

THE "TEST" ANGEL

From *Sara Shockley, Lawson, Missouri:* One day, not long ago, I was driving down the road on my way to Wal-Mart. There was nothing special about the day…nothing special about what I was doing, just a very ordinary day. I was definitely not expecting anything different to happen.

As I was driving, I noticed a shabbily clothed man with a backpack walking on the shoulder of the blacktop in the same direction I was traveling. He was not acting like a hitch-hiker, but was just walking. I didn't even think much about him as I passed him. I glanced back in my rear-view mirror, and he was still trudging along. However, the farther I drove, the more I had this sense that I was supposed to turn around and give him a ride. "No, God," I said, "You can't really mean that," as I drove, trying to put my thoughts back on my shopping trip.

But the feeling persisted and became much stronger

until it almost felt as though it was suffocating me. It seemed as though the Holy Spirit was really making me uncomfortable. It persisted so that I could not dismiss it from my mind. The command to turn around became so strong that I gave in and finally prayed, "Alright, God, if this is from You, just protect me!"

I found a place to turn around and drove back toward the man. By this time he was more than two or three miles from me, but he quickly came into view once more, walking in my direction. I slowed down and had to pass him because he was on the other side of the street. As I did, he looked through the windshield and right into my eyes. I was scared, but when he looked into my eyes, I saw a kindness in them that was unexplainable. All at once, my spirit was filled with a wonderful kind of peace and I was no longer fearful. I knew then that this encounter was from God because I had a total peace like nothing I had ever experienced before.

As I made a U-turn to get on the same side of the road to stop, I had to look back to see if any cars were approaching. He was out of my sight for just a split second. This road was lightly traveled and no one else could be seen either way—just the road, the man, and my car. As I turned back toward the man, suddenly, in the blink of an eye, he had disappeared! No one else could have picked him up. There was no place for him to run to—no nearby homes, buildings, or even deep ditches. He had simply vanished!

I was dumbfounded. It affected me so much that I

pulled off on the shoulder to gather my composure. Nothing in my life had prepared me for this kind of a happening. I just asked: "God why did this happen? What was the purpose in this? What for? Where did he go?"

With this deep peace still in my spirit, the thought struck me that this had been a test to see if I would be faithful, obedient, and willing to do something that would normally fill me with fear. I still don't really know the answer, but as I look back, I do believe it was a test.

The angel of the LORD encamps around those who fear him, and he delivers them (Psalm 34:7).

FOOD FOR THOUGHT: The Bible is full of angel stories, therefore we have no other option than to talk of such beings. The teaching of the Scriptures is that these are created beings who have been chosen to minister in many different kinds of ways. If we are to be faithful students of the Word of God, we have no other choice than to appreciate everything God has made, including angels.

"Christians should never fail to sense the
operation of angelic glory. It forever eclipses
the world of demonic powers, as the
sun does a candle's light."
—*Dr. Billy Graham*

Chapter 5

ANGELS ON GUARD

This happened in East Africa during the Mau Mau uprisings which took place in 1956 and was told to me by Phil Plotts, son of missionary Morris Plotts. Here's the story:

A band of roving Mau Maus came upon the village of Lauri, surrounded it, and killed every inhabitant, including women and children, approximately 300 in all. Not more than three miles away was the "Rift Valley School," a private school where missionary children were being educated. Immediately upon leaving the carnage of Lauri, the Mau Maus came with spears, bows and arrows, clubs, and torches toward the school with the same intentions of complete destruction.

Of course, you can imagine the fear of those little inhabitants and their instructors housed in the boarding school. Word had already reached them about the devastation wreaked upon Lauri. There was no place to flee with the little children and women, and so their only resource was to go to prayer.

Soon, out of the darkness of the night, lighted torches appeared, and quickly a ring of these terrorists circled the school. Shouts and curses could be heard from the Mau Maus as they began to advance. All of a sudden, when they were close enough to throw spears, they stopped and inexplicably began to run the other way!

A call had gone out to the authorities and an army had been sent, but they arrived after the Mau Maus had already left. The army spread out and searched for the rebels until they captured the entire band, including their leaders.

They later appeared before the judge at their trial. The leader was the first one called to the witness stand. The judge questioned: "On this particular night, did you kill the inhabitants of Lauri?"

"Yes."

"Was it your intent to do the same killing at the missionary school in Rift Valley?"

"Yes."

"Well, then," asked the judge, "why did you not complete your mission? Why didn't you attack the school?"

(Allow me to break in upon the story with a note: This Mau Mau leader was a heathen, a person who had never read the Bible, been exposed to Christianity, or told about angels.)

24

The leader replied to the judge: "We were on our way to attack and destroy all the people and the school, but as we came closer, all of a sudden, between us and the school, there were huge men dressed in white and each had a flaming sword. We became afraid and ran to hide."

Later, when the children and instructors were asked if they saw these same men, they all replied with a resounding "no." The missionary in charge of the school hadn't seen any angels, only the flight of the frightened Mau Mau band.

There's a quote from an ancient proverb which says, "When angels come, the devils leave."

For he will command his angels concerning you to guard you in all your ways; they will lift you up in their hands, so that you will not strike your foot against a stone (Psalm 91:11-12).

FOOD FOR THOUGHT: There is no way any of us can fathom how often angels may have been involved in our lives. While angels can become visible, our eyes don't ordinarily see them. It's like not being able to see the dimensions of a nuclear field or the structure of atoms or electricity flowing through a copper wire. Our ability to sense reality is very limited, but that doesn't change the fact that angels have been present!

"But if these beings guard you,
they do so because they have been
summoned by your prayers."
—*Saint Ambrose*

Chapter 6

THE ANGEL
IN THE WINDOW

Evangelist Frankie Walker related the following story to me while I was doing research on angelic visits:

For a season of time, I was removed from my traveling ministry and taught in a Bible school, did some counseling, and was a dorm mother to some 20 girls.

One evening I had to leave the girls for about an hour and a half to pick up a lady who was traveling from another state to visit our church. It was an extremely dark night as I drove from the parking lot. When I was a short distance from the dorm, I sensed a strong presence of fear and the thought came, "I cannot leave the girls alone." I prayed, "Lord, what am I to do? I can't go back, someone has to go to the airport." The Lord impressed me to "charge the angels to guard the dorm." I did this, committing the safety of the girls to the angels.

On arrival back at the dorm, Pastor Eula and I

walked into what should have been a sleeping group of young women. Instead we found all of them seated on the floor, singing and worshipping. The girl in charge met me at the top of the stairs. "I know we are supposed to be in bed, but allow me to tell you why we are not. After you left, we were visiting when another student came home from work. She said, 'Why is Sister Walker standing in her window, curtains open, looking out on the parking lot. She never does that, her curtains are always closed at night.' We laughed at her as we explained she must be seeing things because you had gone to the airport."

She paused to catch her breath and then went on: "We continued talking, then the second carload came from work, the same three girls who ride together each day. One of them asked, 'What is Sister Walker doing with her curtains open, watching the parking lot?' At this, the rest of the girls freaked out, some of them frightened to the point of tears."

They then decided to check into my room. They found the lights off and the drapes closed, just as I had left them. Assured that everything was okay, but still shaken, they began to sing and pray together. All of this had been related to me with eyes wide with excitement and some tears.

Then, I explained to them my experience on the road as I was leaving the parking lot and the instructions to place angels to guard them in my absence.

This was then a wonderful opportunity to explain about the supernatural protection of angels and I said,

"That angel looked like me and was guarding you while I was absent."

James Russell Lowell wrote: "An angel stood and met my gaze, through the low doorway of my tent; the tent is struck, the vision stays; I only know she came and went."

So Peter was kept in prison, but the church was earnestly praying to God for him.... "You're out of your mind," they told her. When she kept insisting that it was so, they said, "It must be his angel" (Acts 12:5, 15).

FOOD FOR THOUGHT: God is sovereign and does what He wants to do, and He does it the way He wants it done. He may use an angel to perform some service at a moment in time. At another time He may use a word of encouragement through a total stranger and the next use a Christian friend to do a kind deed. He can also accomplish His purposes by using neither an angel or a person. Therefore, if the Almighty God can send angels or anybody else to our aid, let's never stop praying for His help in times of need!

"The angels are the dispensers and
administrators of the divine beneficence toward us;
they regard our safety, undertake our defense,
direct our ways and exercise a constant
solicitude that no evil befall us."
—*John Calvin*

Chapter 7

THE GIANT ANGEL

T his story is from Ralph Nicol, a missionary to Mexico. It happened on a state blacktop road on a dark, foggy night in East Texas:

After a church service on a Wednesday night, a man with whom I had been acquainted for a few years approached me with a problem. He needed help in moving his furniture and belongings from his house in Livingston to another house in Chanal View a few miles away, and he knew I had a truck. We drove over to his house and loaded it up with about three hours of hard, sweaty work. By this time I was more than a bit anxious to get on the road and hoped to be back home before morning.

I was in a real hurry as I drove out of Livingston, driving much too fast for the conditions. It was a foggy night, but we were making pretty good time. All I could see was the white center strip and the line on the side of the road that marked where the shoulder began. Yes, it was foolish. Yes, I was going too fast for the conditions. Yes, I was in too much of a hurry. Yes, I knew better, but my desire to get home overcame my sense of caution.

Suddenly, standing directly ahead in the middle of the road, looking back at me over his shoulder was a huge man! He had on bright clothing which glowed through the fog. He was huge and towered over the hood of my truck. I would estimate that he must have been about nine or ten feet tall. He stood still, watching me come up the road. I slammed on the brakes, and the truck burned rubber as it slid to a screeching halt almost on top of him. He smiled at me, and then as we watched, he vanished into thin air, disappearing in an instant! Then it hit both of us—this was an angel on an assignment!

I put the truck in first gear and started down the road, slowly this time, hoping to catch another look at this angel. It was then that we saw a stalled log truck about 100 yards ahead, spread across both sides of the highway. This truck must have pulled out from a side road and stalled, cutting off both lanes of traffic. No flares had yet been put out by the driver because it had just happened. Yes, we were shook up!

I got out and inquired whether the driver needed help, but he was soon able to start the truck up and pulled it to the side of the road. Curious, I went over and asked him if he had seen this strange man. He had not, but he enjoyed the story as I told it to him.

As my friend and I started up the road again, this time

at a much reduced speed, we were talked excitedly about our encounter with a life-saving angel. Soon we were praising God and worshipping One who cared enough about us, even in the midst of our foolishness, to send protection in a time of dire need. Now don't any of you take this as a license to do something foolish in the belief that God will come to your rescue. I don't know why he spared me and my furniture moving friend, but perhaps there was more for us to do to help the kingdom of God.

Even though I walk through the valley of the shadow of death, I will fear no evil, for you are with me; your rod and your staff, they comfort me (Psalm 23:4).

FOOD FOR THOUGHT: Angels don't come to judge us. Their mission is to help and protect us. Sometimes we do foolish things and God sends them to rescue us out of our own foolishness.

"Hush, my dear, lie still and slumber!
Holy angels guard thy bed!
Heavenly blessings without number
Gently falling on thy head."
—*Isaac Watts*

Chapter 8

THE DELIVERY ANGEL

As I look back, I realize that my growing up years were wonderful and idyllic, and I had a really happy childhood. It never dawned on me that life was really tough at times because we were so poor. At this time, my parents were struggling to establish a mission church in west central Minnesota in the town of Evansville, which had a population of about 750 people, not counting dogs and cats. It was not easy to make a living in those days. In addition to being a pioneering pastor, Dad had to work where he could find a job to support the family. Our family consisted of Dad, Mom, my younger brother Gene, who was a year and half my junior, and myself. We had a little garden and ate well when some of the church farm families brought some of their produce to the parsonage. I thought everybody had to live like that, but the memories of those years are good. It's amazing what time can do to memory.

However, one particular night is still a vivid memory.

Mom was setting the table for herself and us two boys when Gene asked, "What are we going to eat tonight?" We had already checked and knew that there was nothing on the stove or in the refrigerator and cupboards, and nothing was on the table except water in the glasses. There was no potato for watery soup or flour with which to make biscuits. There were no noodles for a hot dish of any kind. The house was bare, and two boys were famished!

Mother said, "Let's sit down and ask the Lord to bless our meal." We dutifully bowed our heads and listened to her prayer: "Dear Lord, we thank you because You are so good to us. Bless Dad tonight as he's away working. And, Lord, thank You for the food we are about to partake of, in Jesus' name I pray..." Before she got the final "Amen" said, all three of us heard a noise on the back porch. Being boys, we shoved our chairs back and in a single motion ran for the back door, which was about six steps from the kitchen table, and flung it open. There, sitting on the porch, were boxes of groceries! We ran out onto the porch and down the three steps and looked in every direction up and down our little dirt street. We saw nobody, no car driving away, nothing! Now this is a little country village where everybody knew everybody and everybody knew everybody else's business. We could see quite a distance in all directions, and we could see no one.

You can imagine the great excitement as we hauled the groceries inside, helping Mom put them away until they overflowed the cupboards and the frig! Then we sat down to a glorious feast! We asked, "Mom, who do you think brought the groceries?"

She looked back with a smile and simply said, "Let's just thank the Lord for providing!"

There were other instances of miraculous provision during those same years. Many times some anonymous giver would drop a plain envelope into our mailbox with $50 in it along with a note which simply said: "Let not your right hand know what your left hand is doing." These envelopes always arrived when there was a financial crisis. It was an on-going event which happened many times during those years and they were always delivered on the very day we needed them. Eventually my brother and I set up a watch over our mailbox to catch the person or persons who did it, but never saw anyone put the envelopes in that box.

Rabbah, an ancient Jewish scholar wrote: "Although the span from earth to heaven is a journey of five hundred years, when one whispers a prayer, or even silently meditates, God is nearby and hears."

I was young and now I am old, yet I have never seen the righteous forsaken or their children begging bread (Psalm 37:25).

FOOD FOR THOUGHT: Angels exist for a reason—they are servants of God. They have work to do and apparently always will. Angels exist in numbers so huge they cannot be counted and will be there throughout eternity. Does this give us a hint that heaven will be a busy place with lots of action because God Himself will be setting the pace?

"There are strange ways of serving God,
You sweep a room or turn a sod,
And suddenly, to your surprise,
You hear the whirr of seraphim,
And find you're under God's own eyes
And building palaces for Him."
—*Herman Hagedorn*

Chapter 9

ENTERTAINING THE STRANGER ANGEL

It happened in a logging state, Oregon to be exact, where Eugene and Judy had four kids ranging in age from five to 15. They were a church-going, godly, loving family. Gene had worked at a local lumber mill for years and when it folded, he was forced to do odd jobs for a living. One day he had a small job in town working on a car, and Judy was doing the laundry when some church ladies dropped over for a visit.

Their conversation was broken when Judy's oldest, Wendy, came into the house, "Mom, there's a black man coming around to the back door. Says he's got to talk to you."

Immediately these church ladies warned, "Be careful. Don't have anything to do with a man who's coming begging! Now listen to us!"

At the back door stood the elderly black man with greying hair and soft, warm eyes. "Ma'am, sorry to bother you, but my truck broke down and I'm walking to town. I would appreciate it if you could give me some water and just a bit of food if you could spare it."

Judy was stunned and was hesitant to do the right thing because she had been influenced by the visiting church ladies. Instead of getting the water and food, she stood there. Eyes met and the old man waited a few seconds, and then silently he turned away. Judy felt ashamed as she went back to the table but felt even worse when she saw the condemning look from her oldest son, Drake.

Quickly, she grabbed a pitcher of lemonade and some cookies and ran out the front door to find the old man on his knees with the children around him listening to him telling a Bible story. She offered him the cookies and lemonade and told him to wait and went back inside to prepare a sack lunch. She returned with the lunch and said, "I'm sorry about the way I acted."

"That's all right...too many people are influenced by others. But unlike some, you have overcome it, and this speaks well for you," he replied.

That night, Gene had some wonderful news. The car he had fixed belonged to a man whose brother was looking for a good mechanic for his auto repair shop and so he had hired Gene on the spot! The family had a joyous supper as they celebrated the good news.

Later, after the excitement had died down a bit, Judy related to Gene the events of the afternoon. When she had finished, he asked, "Did you say this was an elderly black man with kind looking eyes and gray hair?"

"Yes."

Gene jumped up from the table and began searching through his pockets until he found a piece of folded paper which he handed to Judy and said, "I met that man walking down the road when I came from town. He waved me over and gave this to me. When I finished reading it for a few short seconds, I looked up to speak with him and he was gone! He had just disappeared—there was no place for him to hide. He simply vanished! I couldn't believe it!"

Judy began to read the note and burst into tears before she had finished reading it. What did the note say? It's our special Bible verse for today: "Do not forget to entertain strangers, for by so doing some people have entertained angels without knowing it!"

Do not forget to entertain strangers, for by so doing some people have entertained angels without knowing it (Hebrews 13:2).

FOOD FOR THOUGHT: If you have never had an angel manifest himself to you, perhaps you can take this as an affirmation of the trust you have placed in God. And if perhaps, in the future God decides it would be wise to dispatch an angel to you or me, don't be surprised. I'm not fixated on angels, but I happen to be convinced that they are far more involved in your world and mine than we may realize.

"Angels descending,
bringing from above,
Echoes of mercy,
whispers of love."
—*Fanny J. Crosby*

Chapter 10

THE MONEY ANGEL

This story begins in the early 1970s, in Rockford, Illinois, as Pastor Don Lyons led his church to purchase some farm land on which to build a new church building and a Christian radio station. First, they built a small house, which was to be used for the radio station if they could manage to get it launched. Pastor Lyons knew they needed to find a special person to manage this start-up ministry. As the pastor prayed about it, in his mind, he could see a name spelled out: "Tietsort." *A most unusual name*, he thought. Shaking his head, he quickly dismissed it from his mind.

Some time later, at a special pastor's meeting for all the churches in Rockford, Pastor Lyons was greeting some of the guests when a young man walked up. The pastor couldn't believe his eyes when he saw the man's name tag, which read: RON TIETSORT! Pastor Lyons soon discovered that Ron had a radio/television background before he became a pastor in Sioux City, Iowa.

Pastor Lyons immediately told the man his story and offered Ron the job of station manager so they could finally get the proposed station on the air. The Tietsort family soon moved to Rockford.

Ron's wife, Millie, became the bookkeeper, receptionist, and occasional programmer. Then in the winter of 1975, reality had to be faced. Despite all their efforts and a growing listener base, the radio station was in deep financial trouble. In order to catch up on their bills and keep it going, the station immediately needed a little more than $3,000, although it might as well have been three million! (Remember at that time a dollar was worth much more than today, and $3,000 seemed like a fortune to them.) By then they had exhausted all possible avenues for fresh revenue. Millie sat looking out the window on a new snowfall, gently falling snow with no wind...a beautiful, refreshing sight. She prayed, "Lord, we really thought You wanted the station to succeed. Did we misread You? Please tell us what to do now."

The front door swung open and a middle-aged man walked in, carrying a sealed envelope. Millie was startled at the sudden intrusion since she had heard no car drive up nor footsteps on the porch. *Perhaps*, she thought, *the snow had muffled the sounds.*

The man said quickly, "Give this to Ron. Use it for the station."

Before Millie could offer him a receipt for tax purposes, he turned and quickly left. Gone! It seemed so strange that the man never engaged in any further conversation with her.

Millie hurried to Ron's office and excitedly plopped the bulging envelope in front of him. With a quizzical look on his face, Ron slit the envelope, opened it, and gasped. "Millie, look!" The envelope was stuffed with money. They quickly began counting it and found the envelope contained $3,250!

Ron leaped from his chair, raced to the front of the house, and flung open the door to call the man back so he could thank him or at least meet him. But there was no car in sight, no tire tracks in the driveway—none coming from the road and none going back out! Then Ron looked down the front walkway and saw there were also no footprints! He looked at the fresh snow on the unshoveled front porch, and it was completely smooth. There was nothing to be seen anywhere on the fresh white carpet of clean snow!

Well, what about today? Yes, Station WQFL and its companion station of WGLS are still operating!

And Ron and Millie never saw the stranger again, but how well they remember him.

H.C. Moolenburgh wrote: "The farther we go along the path of God, the more angels we shall encounter."

And my God will meet all your needs according to his glorious riches in Christ Jesus (Philippians 4:19).

FOOD FOR THOUGHT: If you are a Bible student, you no doubt have discovered impressive evidence of what angels did throughout the biblical accounts. But you may be thinking, "What evidence is there today that angels are still doing such things?" The place to start is with the character of God who has His reasons for creating angels (as well as you and me), and they all come from who He is!

"The golden moments in the stream of life
rush past us and we see nothing but sand;
the angels come to visit us, and we only
know them when they are gone."
—*George Eliot*

Chapter 11

HOW DO YOU VERIFY
AN ANGEL STORY?

The George Steen family was traveling on I-35 through Iowa in a blinding snowstorm. As they drove, the storm intensified. Although travel was slow and harrowing, they decided to keep on going, thinking they might drive out of it near the Missouri border. But their real concern at the moment was the gas gauge in their Lincoln—it was showing empty! The storm had closed down just about everything, including gas stations.

The family prayed for help. It was critical that they find fuel, so at the next small town exit they turned off and went in search of help. The town's police officer stopped, and upon learning of their plight, told them to follow him to a station where he had the key and could get them some gas. They followed him and were able to fill up their gas tank. He refused their offer to pay for the gas, and they drove off. They had not gone far when one of the girls said, "We didn't really thank the man properly." They all agreed and turned around and headed back, only to find it was an abandoned station, obviously not in service for years! Then, they drove around looking for the officer and stopped a person to inquire about where the town cop could be found, only to be told that they did not have a town cop!

Now the question we're going to tackle in this chapter is, "How do you verify an angel story?" As you've been reading this book or any other book on angels, did you ever wonder, "How can these angel stories be verified?" Well, I know I have.

Of course, the Bible records many incidents concerning the ministry of angels and their supernatural help. And the authority of the Bible speaks for itself and is beyond question. But how can you verify the story of someone who claims to have had an angelic encounter? The bottom line is that we must depend solely upon our sources—the people involved who experienced them—because many of these incidents cannot be documented in any other way.

Perhaps the very reason why we have doubts is that we must depend on the honesty and integrity of the people sharing their experience. Maybe this is one of the reasons why some people who have had angelic happenings are reluctant to share it. If we believe in the possibility of supernatural interventions, we must also have faith in our fellow human beings who have experienced them.

Yes, you can discount any of these stories, and shoot holes through any of them, but as you do, the thoughts are always there: It could have really happened; it could be true! So trust is part of believing. As I write this book, I have taken each of these stories at face value without judging or thinking, "This is absurd." I've shared them as they have been shared with me by people of integrity, and you are the judge!

Consider this: Gladys Triplett barely had the strength to answer the doorbell one morning in 1941 in Newberg, Oregon. Not completely recovered from the birth of her eighth child, she had spent another sleepless night; and although it was only 10:30 am, she was exhausted. She felt too weak to tackle the pile of dirty dishes, unmade beds, and huge laundry pile and could expect no help from her husband because he had been called out town.

Gladys finally made it to the door and opened it to a plainly dressed woman who said: "The Father has sent me to minister to you because of your distress and great need. You called with all your heart, and you asked in faith."

Lifting Gladys, the stranger laid her on the couch and said, "Your heavenly Father heard your prayer. Sleep now my child." When Gladys awoke three hours later, feeling refreshed and healed, the change in the house was amazing! Dishes were done, floors were clean, toys picked up, the baby had been bathed and was sleeping, the dining room table was set, food for dinner had been prepared, all the laundry was done, and even the ironing finished!

Who was the woman? Gladys said that no human being could have done so much in only three hours!

Okay, my reader friend, what do you think? How do you verify this story? How about a simple prayer of thanksgiving offered to a heavenly Father who really cares about His hurting children? And take the story at face value and rejoice in it!

> *...but Mary stood outside the tomb crying. As she wept, she bent over to look into the tomb and saw two angels in white, seated where Jesus' body had been, one at the head and the other at the foot* (John 20:11-12).

FOOD FOR THOUGHT: Angels are God's servants, just like many of the biblical characters—John, John the Baptist, Amos, Daniel, Ezekiel and more. In fact, aren't we all to be a servant of God when we speak a word of testimony on His behalf or when we offer a cup of cold water in His name? "Servant" is one of the most commonly used titles in the Bible for those who follow the Lord. Observe the ministry of angels...aren't they true servants?

"Therefore look behind the screen,
Trust the powers of the Unseen.
Neither vague nor mystical
Are our friends angelical."
—*Amy Carmichael*

Chapter 12

HEAVYWEIGHT ANGELS

My mother related this story about another ministry couple who were contemporaries of theirs when they were pastors in Minnesota. The now deceased Pastor and Mrs. B.C. Heinz were the ministry family at a small church in North Dakota.

The Heinzes and another couple from their church made their way to a late spring-time fellowship meeting quite a distance away in the town of Dickinson, where Pastor Heinz was to be one of the scheduled speakers. This happened to be one of those all-day affairs—morning service, lunch, afternoon meeting, a minister's business meeting, dinner, and finally the evening rally/service. When it was all finished, it was approximately 10:30 pm as the couple drove away from the church. Springtime weather in North Dakota can be very unpredictable. They turned north on state Highway 85 towards Williston, and about that time it started to rain, sleet, snow, and freeze all at the same time.

They started down into the valley and the icy mixture continued to fall but with a greater intensity. It began to accumulate on the highway, making driving very treacherous and the visibility near zero. They had no snow tires or chains on the car because it was late spring and they hadn't anticipated any more snow. Mrs. Heinz began to pray: "Help us, Lord, help our car, keep us safe."

As they began the climb from the valley floor, the car began to lose traction and soon they came to a complete stop. No matter what they tried, the car would spin out of control, since they had absolutely no traction on the freezing gunk. There was nothing more they could do but prepare to spend the night huddled in the car, waiting for the snowplow or other help to come their way. The prospects of spending the freezing night there were not very pleasant.

About this time a car drove up behind them with six husky young men in it. They stopped behind the stalled car and one of them asked if they could be of help. Pastor Heinz said, "A push would help us but what we really need is more traction on the rear end, perhaps more weight would help us make it to the top."

The pastor started the car and five of these young men began to push the car up the steep snow covered road. As soon as it began rolling, they all jumped up on the trunk. Two were sitting with their feet dangling over the sides and the other three were sitting facing the rear with their feet on the rear bumper. With this help, the car easily made it to the top of the hill.

Pastor Heinz immediately stopped the car and got out to thank the kind heavyweight strangers. When he stepped out of the car to speak with the men, he discovered that they had all disappeared! There was not a trace of them nor of the car in which they had come that had followed them to the top of the hill—not even a tire track!

Billy Graham writes: "Reports continually flow to my attention from many places around the world telling of visitors of the angelic order appearing, ministering, fellowshipping, and disappearing."

But you have come to Mount Zion, to the heavenly Jerusalem, the city of the living God. You have come to thousands upon thousands of angels in joyful assembly, to the church of the firstborn, whose names are written in heaven. You have come to God, the judge of all men, to the spirits of righteous men made perfect... (Hebrews 12:22-23).

FOOD FOR THOUGHT: Catching a glimpse of angels doesn't depend completely on what form God assigns to them. The Bible strongly supports the concept that the Lord must open our eyes before we can see them. Take the case of Daniel and his companions near the Tigris River: one person saw the angel but the people next to him didn't. Or take the time that a donkey could see the angel, but the person riding the donkey could not.

"Outside the open window
The morning air is all awash with angels."
—*Richard Wilbur*

Chapter 13

THE BUS RIDING ANGEL

From North Mankato, Minnesota: Two things are always in short supply when you are a college student: sleep and money to go home with. Margarete was away at college, a hard working, diligent, college sophomore. She was a resident of a dorm where sleep was in short commodity. Girls being girls, and studies being studies, and boys being subjects of many late night conversations, the nights seemed pretty short.

The Christmas holidays were soon approaching, which meant a trip home was almost in sight. But as always, college professors haven't much heart and usually schedule tests on the last three or four days preceding vacation. So again, sleep was hard to come by.

Grandma Hendley had sent the funds for Margarete's long bus ride home. As soon as the last class was over, Margarete made her way to the bus depot loaded down with packages and a few presents she had purchased. She quickly purchased her ticket and boarded the bus.

She was thankful that her first choice in seats was available—the very last seat next to the back door—where she could stretch out and sleep without interruption all the way to her destination of Mankato, Minnesota.

It felt like such a luxury for her to be able to stretch out with no one to bother her with questions or break into her sleep. The only sounds that filled the bus were those of the other passengers quietly murmuring to each other and the steady humming of the tires on the highway. Such were the comforting, soothing sounds that lulled a tired college sophomore to sleep.

As she slept, the motion of the bus and her tossing pushed her shoulders against the back door. Suddenly, without warning, the back emergency exit door swung open with Margarete wedged against it! Her head and shoulders hung out the open door, awakening her instantly, of course, and she felt herself falling into the blackness of the night towards the hard concrete of the highway. Her first thought was *I'm going to die!* She frantically grabbed for the door frame to catch herself but missed!

She prayed the most fervent prayer of her short life in was just three words: "Jesus, help me!"

And to this day, she says she can almost still feel it— a pair of huge hands caught her and pushed her back into the bus! She quickly looked around, but no one was sitting near enough to her to have touched her!

When the warning light of the open door flashed red, the driver brought the bus to a quick stop and came running down the aisle to check on the problem. Stopping short, he quickly took in the sight of Margarete sitting next to the open door and leaned down to ask her, "Are you all right? I can't understand how it happened. Did you lose anything? Are you afraid? Did you get hurt?" As you can imagine, he was more than a bit upset with the problem.

Still in a sort of shock, Margarete answered, "No sir, no problems."

"Well, then, how did you manage to hold on and not fall out?"

She replied, "I believe I had some heavenly help."

When you pass through the waters, I will be with you; and when you pass through the rivers, they will not sweep over you. When you walk through the fire, you will not be burned; the flames will not set you ablaze. For I am the LORD, your God, the Holy One of Israel, your Saviour; I give Egypt for your ransom, Cush and Seba in your stead (Isaiah 43:2-3).

FOOD FOR THOUGHT: Angels are real, but not made of material substances like we are. Apparently, they have no physical nature, not even breath or blood. If they do occupy some form of permanent body it has to be a spiritual body—apparently just like the spiritual body we shall occupy some day in eternity!

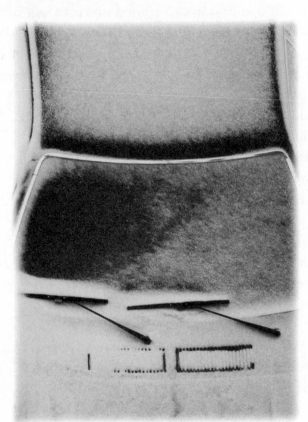

"Do you think that I cannot appeal
to My Father, and He will at once
send me more than twelve
legions of angels?"
—*Matthew 26:53*

Chapter 14

ANGELS IN THE SNOW

When you live in Colorado, especially in or near the mountains, or have to cross them in the wintertime, you learn how to travel with precautions such as extra clothing, a survival kit, tire chains, snow shovel, etc. What happens when you are caught without these precautions?

Well, J.D. and his family are native to Colorado and live in Grand Junction on the western slope of the Rocky Mountains. In late August one year, they were returning home from a trip and had to cross Red Mountain Pass from Durango to Grand Junction. It was still summertime and so their car wasn't equipped for winter travel as yet. They were making their climb over the pass, which is 11,008 feet in elevation on the top. This highway is named the "Million Dollar Highway" because of the great cost per mile to originally build it. It's one of the most treacherous roads to travel, even in good weather, full of steep grades and hairpin turns but without many guardrails. When the weather is wet, snowy, or icy, the road is downright dangerous and often closed to travel.

J.D.'s family was traveling the road with their three little children. As they neared the top, they noticed a dense cloud cover and a storm brewing, but didn't think too much about it. As they topped out at the summit and started down the other side, they immediately found themselves in a late summer's snowstorm! Wind was blowing the heavy snow, making it freeze to an icy glaze on the roadway. Visibility was poor, but there was no place to turn around or stop. All they could do was to proceed as cautiously as possible in navigating the ice-covered, slick hairpin turns and steep downhill grade. Conditions worsened quickly. The first thing they did was to pray. As J.D. drove, his wife Agnes and the kids were praying.

In spite of all J.D.'s careful precautions and down-shifting, the car began to slip and slide. The edge of the road, with no guardrail to protect drivers at this stretch, came extremely close. The car continued to skid towards the edge and the hundreds of feet drop to the distant valley below.

All of a sudden, two men appeared running beside the car—one with his hand on the left front fender and the other on the left rear fender. The car straightened out of the skid and these two men continued to run alongside of the car until J.D. had maneuvered it through the last treacherous, icy hairpin curve to enter the town of Ouray.

J.D. pulled the car over to the side of the road and stopped in order to thank the men who had come to their rescue. But as he got out of the car, no one was to be found! There was no place for the men to go but up or down the mountain road which could clearly be seen in both directions. The family looked but there were not even any footprints in the snow!

Safely down the mountain, they expressed their thanksgiving to the Lord for His protection and care in sending the two men who had come to their rescue.

Joseph Glanvill noted that, "What's impossible to all humanity may be possible to the metaphysics and physiology of angels."

The angel of the LORD encamps around those who fear him, and he delivers them (Psalm 34:7).

FOOD FOR THOUGHT: One thing we do know is that angels are God's representatives, messengers ordered by God to help in countless ways. They also protect us in ways we are not aware of. In fact, none of us has any idea of how many times an angel has been there to protect us. Some day in heaven, it will be exciting to see how many times angels were there when we needed them!

"All God's angels come
to us disguised."
—*James Russell Lowell*

Chapter 15

ANGEL STORIES FROM AROUND THE WORLD

DURING WORLD WAR II, Wayne was the navigator on a B-24 bomber and stationed in Italy. On one particular bombing run over central Europe, as they were approaching the target area, he felt a strong hand on his shoulder and heard a voice which said, "Get up and go to the back of the plane!" He immediately responded, and in the brief amount of time he spent walking to the back and returning, they took some anti-aircraft fire. When Wayne took his place back in the cockpit, he noticed that a shell had blown a hole in the ceiling of the plane and had come right up through his navigator's seat!

———

SIX SOVIET COSMONAUTS said they witnessed a most awe-inspiring spectacle in space—a band of glowing angels! According to *Weekly World News*, cosmonauts Vladimir Solovev, Oleg Atkov, and Leonid Kizim said they first saw the celestial beings during their 155th day aboard the orbiting "Salyat Seven" space station. "What we saw," they said, "were seven giant figures in the form of humans but with wings and mist-like halos, as in the classic depiction of angels." Twelve days later, the figures returned and were seen by three other Soviet scientists, including woman cosmonaut Svetlann Savitskaya who said, "They were smiling, as though they shared in a glorious secret."

———

THIS NEXT STORY IS RELATED BY A PASTOR who had gone to Mexico on a preaching mission: While we were returning, our van developed mechanical problems. After jacking up the van, I crawled under to check out the problem, and the jack collapsed! There was a crushing force against my chest, and my traveling companions quickly grabbed the bumper to lift the van, but weren't able to lift it.

I then cried out, "Jesus! Jesus!" Within seconds, a youthful looking Mexican young man came running to the van. He was thin and small, but his face was smiling. As he reached the van, he grabbed the bumper and lifted it like a feather. As I was freed, I was pulled out by my companions and felt my chest expand and the broken bones mend. The visitor then lowered the van, waved to us and ran in the direction from which he had come until he disappeared on the horizon!

A SEVENTY-YEAR-OLD CHINESE LADY was the only person who had knowledge of the daily operations of her family, as well as the operations of their house church, which had to operate underground because of persecution in China. The lady alone knew where the Bibles were hidden, who the messengers were, and who could be trusted. Unfortunately, she died suddenly of a heart attack! The family was lost because she had not been able to pass on her important information. They began to pray: "Lord, restore our mother back to life." After being dead for two days, she came back to life and scolded her family for calling her back to life because she didn't want to return. They reasoned with her that after she had given them the much-needed information, they would pray for her to go back to heaven.

After two days during which she shared with them everything they needed to know, the family and friends began to sing hymns and pray that the Lord would take her back! The mother's final words were: "They're coming! Two angels are coming!" This incident caused an entire village to become Christian!

ONCE WHEN JOHN G. PATON WAS A MISSIONARY in the New Hebrides Islands, hostile natives surrounded his mission headquarters one night and were intent on burning the Patons out and killing them. Terror-stricken, Paton and his wife prayed throughout the night. At dawn, just as their would-be attackers neared the building, the couple was amazed to see the attackers suddenly turn and flee.

A year later, the chief of that hostile tribe was converted to Christianity. Paton asked him what had kept him and his men from burning down the house and killing them on that fateful night. In response, the chief asked Paton a question: "Who were all those men you had with you there?" Paton told him that there was just he and his wife. But the chief insisted they had seen hundreds of men standing guard—big men in shining garments with drawn swords!

He then added, "I tell you the truth, you shall see heaven open, and the angels of God ascending and descending on the Son of Man" (John 1:51).

FOOD FOR THOUGHT: We may never experience the supernatural deliverance of an angel, but God promises us supernatural power and strength of spirit at all times to build our faith and trust in Him and strengthen our character. In such experiences, we learn what Jesus meant when He said, "Blessed are those who have not seen and yet have believed."

"Miracles do not happen in contradiction
to nature, but only in contradiction to that
which is known to us of nature."
—*St. Augustine*

Chapter 16

MIRACLE UNDER THE HOOD

The origins of a story often cannot be traced. The following one, which was told to a nationwide TV audience by the late Howard Conatser, founder of the Beverly Hills Baptist Church of Dallas, Texas is one of those stories.

I do not recall their names, so we'll call these two teenage sisters Karen and Susan. They had been shopping in a suburban mall, and when they were ready to leave, they were chagrined to find that it was already dark outside. Their father had told them to come home before dark. From the mall exit they saw their car, the only one left in that particular section of the parking lot.

They were nervous and hesitant to go out the door. They stood waiting, hoping some other customers would come along so they could all walk out together. The girls were aware of the current crime wave in area shopping malls and remembered their dad's final warning as they left the house: "Don't stay too late!"

"Let's get with it...now!" Susan shifted her packages, pushed open the door, and walked as fast as she could with Karen following. Both were looking from side to side as they quickly made their way to the car. Karen shoved the key into the door lock, hastily got in, and reached across to open Susan's door when they both heard the sound of running feet coming towards them from behind. They turned to look and panicked because racing toward their car were two ominous looking men!

One of the men shouted, "We got you, you're not going anywhere!"

Susan jumped in and both locked their doors just in time. With shaking hands, Karen turned the ignition switch. Nothing happened! She tried again and again—still nothing! Not even a click! They looked at each other with the sinking knowledge that they had no power. The men approached with tire irons in hand, ready to smash a window.

The girls knew they had but scant seconds of safety left, so they grabbed each other's hands and prayed! "Dear God," Susan pleaded, "give us a miracle in the name of Jesus!"

Again Karen turned the key, and the engine roared to life! They raced out of the parking lot, squealing their tires and leaving their astonished would-be attackers behind.

The girls cried all the way home, shocked and yet relieved. They screeched into the driveway, pulled the car into the garage, burst into the house, and spilled out their story in quick gasps. Their parents held them close and comforted their frightened daughters.

"You're safe, thank God, that's the main thing. But don't do it again," Dad said. Then their father frowned, "It's strange. That car has never failed to start. I'll just take a look at it now."

In the garage he raised the hood, and in one stunned glance, he realized who had brought his daughters home safely that night for there was no battery in the car!

The men were amazed and asked, "What kind of man is this? Even the winds and the waves obey him!" (Matthew 8:27)

FOOD FOR THOUGHT: Angels have carried out all kinds of assignments recorded in the Bible, from guarding the entrance to the Garden of Eden, feeding Elijah, healing Isaiah's lips, freeing Peter from prison, to guiding John around the New Jerusalem. Protection and deliverance seem to be regular types of assignments for them. Now the question: Has God assigned one particular angel to take care of just you? Lots of folks think that all of us have guardian angels.

"Angels guard you when you walk with Me.
What better way could you choose?"
—*Frances J. Roberts*

Chapter 17

THE RESCUING ANGEL

A lady from the state of Montana had traced me down and phoned to share her story. This was a story, she said, that no one else knew about other than her parents, not even her husband. She decided to give me permission to use it in case it might encourage someone else.

This woman was eight years old when the story happened. She and three other neighbor kids were playing together in the street in front of their homes. One thing led to another and pretty soon they were participating in an activity which had been forbidden. Forbidden fruit that has some risk attached seems to increase the excitement. Parked in the street was a 1940 Ford coupe with a long sloping trunk, and they began climbing up on the top and sliding down the trunk. It was her turn once again and down she came, dead center on the trunk and impaled herself on the middle bumper guard, which pierced through and into her vagina and rectum.

Immediately she screamed in pain and the blood flowed freely. The other neighbor kids became really scared and ran away leaving her alone and unable to free herself.

"Almost immediately," she told me, "a man dressed in a beautiful gray suit, white shirt, and tie came running up to the car. He reached down and lovingly, carefully lifted me off the bumper guard. He talked to me in a comforting tone of voice, telling me that I would be all right. The pain, which had been unbearable, quickly stopped as he carried me to our front door. He knocked on the door and my mother answered. She was understandably upset with the sight of so much blood on my dress, legs, socks, and shoes. The man gently said, 'You should take her to your doctor to be examined.' Then he handed me over to my mother's arms and left.

"My mother quickly carried me out to our car, hopped in the front seat and backed down the driveway and into the street for the short trip to the emergency room. But before she shifted gears to proceed, she stopped and got out, thinking she should express her thanks to the kind man, but he was nowhere to be found. At the hospital they carefully examined me and could find nothing wrong nor was there any part of my body hurt. Yes, they saw all the blood, and I explained what had happened and they just shook their heads. They sent me home with a very grateful mother.

"Years passed, but my mother was always concerned about any internal injuries I may have sustained. But everything seemed to function normally for a growing girl. After I was married, she was concerned whether or not I could have children, but that was happily settled, too. Today I am the mother of three healthy kids and a happily married woman with no female problems of any kind!

"I've often thought about that kind man in the gray suit. The only conclusion I have come to is that it was an angel on assignment. Following that hospital visit, my mother had inquired if anyone had seen such a man in our small town where everybody knew about everybody else and their business, but found no one who had." Before hanging up the phone, she thanked me for listening to her story so that someone else might be encouraged.

Praise the LORD, you his angels, you mighty ones who do his bidding, who obey his word. Praise the LORD, all his heavenly hosts, you his servants who do his will (Psalm 103:20-21).

FOOD FOR THOUGHT: We must remember that the object of our faith is the most important, and that object is to be God. Would you trust and love Him more if you were to see an angel today? We are to love Him even if we have never seen an angel or experienced an angelic visit or deliverance. God desires us to love Him for who He is, not because He has angels at His command.

"Far beyond the shifting screen
Made of things that can be seen,
Are our friends angelical
Of the land celestial."
—*Amy Carmichael*

Chapter 18

MORE THAN ONE ENCOUNTER

Are you one of those people who has been reading this book and asking yourself why you haven't had an angelic visit? Sometimes life experiences just don't seem fair. I'm sorry, but there is no method known to man that can guarantee you an angelic visit. However, note the following, especially as they are all experiences of the same lady, *Jenith Neselroad, Lawson, Missouri.*

The first experience: It happened in 1955 in Richmond, Missouri. One day there was a knock at my front door at approximately 2:00 pm on a warm summer day. When I answered the door, there was a man standing there who seemed to be very ordinary looking, and who was plainly but neatly dressed. In a quiet voice he said, "This is yours" and handed me a box. I quickly looked inside and discovered a white Bible with a gold cross on the cover and a zipper on three sides of it, quite an attractive object.

I told him, "I can't pay you for it" and gave it back to him.

He replied with the same short sentence, "This is yours" and once more thrust it into my hands.

Again I said, "I can't pay you for it."

And once again he replied, "This is yours" and turned and walked off the porch.

It had been a strange encounter. I watched him as he stepped off the porch and then simply vanished! I never saw where he went; he was just gone. There was no car parked in front of the house nor could I see one anywhere. He had disappeared!

I was not a Christian at this time, but later I accepted the Lord Jesus Christ as my personal Savior. No one ever came back to ask me to pay for the Bible, and I was never sent a bill for it. It had to be one of God's angels on a mission to deliver a copy of the Bible to an unbeliever.

The second experience: This time I was attempting to get away from a car that was following me. I was frightened. It was around 11:00 pm on a dark night and I began crying out to God to send me an angel for protection. I stopped in front of the Christian Union Church because it was lighted at night. The other car skidded to a stop behind me, waited a short time, and suddenly backed up and quickly drove off. Later, I discovered the identity of the one who had been following me and learned that he had been intent on doing me harm.

Apparently he was prevented from doing so because he saw a man riding with me. Then I realized he had seen my guardian angel whom God had sent.

The third experience: One Sunday morning I attended the Nazarene Church in Lawson, Missouri. It was lightly snowing on my way there, but as we sat in church, I could see it really began to snow hard. I had one snow tire and one regular tire on the rear. I prayed all through church for some kind of help so I could return home in safety. I would have to climb a steep hill to get there and knew if I stopped or slowed at any time, I would slide off in the ditch. This was my only way home, and I was really frightened.

I left church in the snowstorm, and the roads had already become slick. The way was so treacherous because I needed speed to make it up the hill but once at the top there was a sharp left turn up another hill. The road was difficult in good conditions, let alone in the middle of a snowstorm. I prayed continuously as I started up the hill. When I managed to reach the top, there was a man dressed in a black suit stopping the traffic coming my way in the other lane. He motioned for me to hurry and not stop on the hill and to continue up the next hill. I made it! As I rounded the left turn I looked in my rear view mirror and there was no man in black directing traffic. That lane of traffic was moving and had not stopped!

The angel of the LORD encamps around those who fear him, and he delivers them (Psalm 34:7).

FOOD FOR THOUGHT: Why do some people experience angels and others can go a lifetime without having that kind of experience? I don't have the answer. Maybe some of us don't need angelic protection as much as others. I know that's not a good answer, either. We must remember that God is sovereign and can do what He pleases including sending an angel when the situation requires. The Christian walk is always an exercise in faith.

"An angel can illumine the thought
and mind of man by strengthening the power
of vision, and by bringing within his
reach some truth which the angel
himself contemplates."
—*St. Thomas Aquinas*

Chapter 19

THE VANISHING HITCHHIKER

W hen doing research about angels or interviewing people about angelic encounters, there is one recurring kind of story which pops up everywhere with all kinds of adaptations or variations. Practically every book on angels includes a version. You may even know of someone who has had such an experience.

Pastor Mark Hernandez was on his way to make a call on a sick member of his church, and there was a 15 mile stretch of barren land through which he had to drive. On this stretch he stopped to pick up a young hitchhiker. There was nothing special about the young man—he was simply dressed but neat and clean. He seemed very pleasant with a wonderful smile that he fastened on the pastor when he stopped the car. It was a common western courtesy to always stop to help anyone who might be in need in such a desolate place. The pastor did not notice a car or other means of transportation nearby, which was a bit unusual, and wondered how the man happened to be on such a lonely stretch alone. But as they drove along, the pastor began to talk with the young man about the love of Jesus Christ.

Pastor Hernandez made this statement in the course of conversation: "I believe the Lord's return is getting very close."

The young man softly, yet forcefully, replied, "Well, that will be sooner than you think." This reply surprised the pastor.

They continued driving and the young man continued, "Please make sure you are ready and all of your congregation also gets this warning."

The pastor thought about the unusual message he has just been given and the strange presence of the young man in the middle of nowhere. He began to sense some kind of special occurrence was happening, but he kept his eyes on the road as he drove.

After a bit of silence, Pastor Hernandez turned to look at his passenger, but the young man had vanished! He stopped the car, got out and looked up and down the lonely road, but was unable to see anyone in any direction in the deserted stretch of Arizona countryside.

Emidio John Pepe wrote: "He has His reasons for doing what He does, and He will explain them to us someday."

But the angel said to them, "Do not be afraid. I

bring you good news of great joy that will be for all the people" (Luke 2:10).

FOOD FOR THOUGHT: Are such angel sightings the real thing? What does this tell us about God's messengers and how they appear and how they relay a message? More importantly, how can such sightings help draw us closer than ever to the God we serve?

"There is rejoicing in the presence
of the angels of God over one
sinner who repents."
—*Luke 15:10*

Chapter 20

THE ANGEL TRUCK DRIVER

The following story was related to me but the circumstances, names, and location have been changed.

It happened in a small town and a church in a farming area in a mid-western state. Pastor Vernon Anderson was a good leader, considered to be the pastor of the entire community, and was wonderful man. His church was thriving and growing, and he used a number of lay people to assist in many ways. Among these volunteers was a man who was the worship leader and was well known in the congregation and the community. Sometimes difficult things happen. This worship leader was discovered to be having an extra-marital affair with another woman. When this sin was uncovered, the pastor immediately dismissed him from his duties of leading the congregation in worship.

The man reacted in anger when informed, and among some of the things he said to the pastor was this statement: "I'll get you for this if it's the last thing I do!" After this declaration, he stomped out of the pastor's office and slammed the door.

The next day, the pastor was driving out of the church parking lot in his pickup and was stopped by this irate man named Tom. As the man approached the truck, Pastor Anderson reached across the seat and took his 24 ounce framing hammer from the tool box and held it in his lap, just in case. Tom threatened him again but did him no harm, just verbally venting his anger at the pastor for making him an example and accusing him of exposing his affair for the whole town to see.

Later the next day, Pastor Anderson received a phone call from Tom. This time Tom seemed calm and asked if he could meet the pastor to offer an apology for his behavior. The pastor agreed, and Tom named the place. They were to meet on the top of a hill on a gravel road about four miles out of town. The pastor really didn't think too much about the location, but was grateful for the opportunity to make things right between them.

At the appointed time, the pastor drove out of town on the gravel road and stopped on the hilltop where they were supposed to meet. He got out of his pickup to wait for Tom and soon saw the dust cloud behind Tom's truck, coming fast in his direction. Tom slammed on his brakes and skidded to a stop behind the pastor's pickup. At almost the same time and from the opposite direction came a brand new, red, Chevrolet water truck that pulled to the side of the road, opposite the pastor and Tom.

Tom took one look at the red truck, jumped into his own truck, spun it around, and spewed gravel in all directions as he beat a track back in the direction from which he had come. The pastor watched him disappear into the distance and turned to talk with the driver of the water truck, but both it and the driver had disappeared. He could see a couple of miles in both directions from the top of the hill and there was no tank truck or driver to be seen!

Later, when the pastor asked the man who delivered water in their town if he had purchased a new truck, he was told that the man still drove his old one.

A few days later, the pastor received another call from Tom who asked, "Why did you have that other truck come when I was to meet you?"

Pastor Anderson replied, "I don't know who it was or where it came from. He just drove up."

Tom continued, "I wanted to meet you on that hill because nobody is ever around there, and I planned to kill you."

Yes, Tom did eventually apologize and asked forgiveness. He repented and became a part of church life again. The pastor, to this day, hopes to see the red water tank truck once more. He told me that because of the rural setting he can recognize everybody's vehicle in a quite a large area, but no one ever had a red truck with a stainless steel tank!

And Elisha prayed, "O LORD, open his eyes so that he may see." Then the LORD opened the servant's eyes, and he looked and saw the hills full of horses and chariots of fire all round Elisha (II Kings 6:17).

FOOD FOR THOUGHT: Jean Paul Richter said, "The guardian angels of life sometimes fly so high as to be beyond our sight, but they are always looking down upon us." How many times have you been delivered from danger and have not even been aware of your angelic protection?

"See, I am sending an angel ahead of you
to guard you along the way and to bring you
to the place I have prepared. Pay attention
to him and listen to what he says."
—*Exodus 23:20-21*

Chapter 21

PROTECTION IN ISRAEL

Here is another story from Reverend Frankie Walker, who shared earlier about the girls being protected in their dorm:

I was released from a Bible school in Virginia in August of 1990 to go to my next assignment in Israel. The Gulf War seemed like it might go full-scale, and Saddam Hussein was threatening Israel at this time. President H.W. Bush had encouraged the American people to stay away from Israel because it was not uncommon to have two or three car and bus bombings each week along with other senseless killings. Many of these bombings were targeted at blue-eyed, blonde-haired people. Americans, or those who looked like Americans, were targets. I must say that it is always of importance for missionaries to be directed and guided by the Holy Spirit because it's a significant factor in their protection.

I was not afraid during the entire three and one-half

months I was there, but I was always in tune with the leading and the inner voice of the Holy Spirit and sensed the presence of angels with me at all times.

The following experience, only one of many, happened in Jerusalem. I had traveled there from Rehovot, where I was living at the time and which was approximately an hour's bus ride away. I had gone to Jerusalem many times and stayed there, sometimes for days at a time.

I had not been able to go to the Upper Room, where all Christian tourists want to go, because of the prevalent danger; but nevertheless, I was determined to make a visit there. One Sunday after church, I headed for the Damascus Gate but one block away from where I was to make the turn to go there, I had a very strong impression that I was to go instead to the YMCA for tea. I had learned to rely on such promptings, so I immediately proceeded to the YMCA. I ordered tea and had been sitting there for a short time when some Europeans came and sat at the table next to me.

In a loud and clear voice I overheard one man say, "I'm glad we were not inside the Damascus Gate when the riots broke out." Then another added, "They had all those home-made bombs and the knives and rocks were flying. They destroyed the police booth and locked out the police that had come to reinforce the soldiers who were inside."

Praise welled up inside of me. If I had not been in

tune with the Spirit of God, I could have been injured or killed like so many others who were there that day.

Then Frankie finishes with this admonition: "Obedience is a must for all of God's children who might travel to dangerous places because your very life may depend upon it."

The Son of Man will send out his angels, and they will weed out of his kingdom everything that causes sin and all who do evil (Matthew 13:41).

FOOD FOR THOUGHT: One of the major recurring themes of angelic interventions is that of protection. This brings up the thought that God doesn't need protection so why did He create troops of heavenly messengers? The theologian Calvin says: "In creating angels, God must have had our interests in mind. God employs angels simply as a help to our weakness, in order to elevate our hopes or strengthen our confidence."

"In this dim world of clouding cares,
We rarely know, till 'wildered eyes
See white wings lessening up the skies,
The Angels with us unawares."
—*Gerald Massey*

Chapter 22

THE SECRET AGENT ANGEL

This story was told by Billy Graham to a group of ministers prior to a city-wide crusade. I was in that group of ministers and heard this story, which I share to the best of my ability:

"When I (Dr. Graham), was visiting some of the American troops during the Korean conflict, I was told of a small group of U.S. Marines who had been trapped in the north and cut off from the rest of their company. The thermometer plunged to near twenty degrees below zero, and they were close to freezing to death and had had nothing to eat for six days. Their only way out was to surrender to the Chinese, so it seemed.

"But one of these Marines, a Christian, related a number of scriptures for encouragement and also taught his fellow Marines to sing a song of praise and worship to God. Following this, they heard a crashing noise in the brush and snow. They turned to see a wild boar running toward them! As they were attempting to jump out of his way, he stopped dead in his tracks! One of the

Marines managed to grab his rifle to shoot it, but before he could get the shot off, the boar toppled over. They immediately rushed at him to kill him with their knives, only to find him dead! That night they feasted on pork roast, pork chops, and were able to cook hams to regain their strength.

"The next morning at sunrise, they heard another noise coming through the woods. They immediately feared that a Chinese patrol had stumbled upon them, but this fear vanished as they found themselves facing a South Korean who spoke fluent English. With a bright smile he said, "I will show you the way out." He led them through the forest and mountains until they reached safety back behind the American lines. When they looked up to thank him, they found he had disappeared!"

The psalmist, David, who knew a thing or two about protection in battles, wrote these comforting words: "He who dwells in the shelter of the Most High will rest in the shadow of the Almighty... For He will command His angels concerning you to guard you in all your ways; they will lift you up in their hands..." (Psalm 91:1, 11-12)

Much more recently, this story made news in Southern California. A child was playing with the handle of a car door as his mother and her sister drove on a California freeway with six lanes of traffic in one direction. The door came open and the child fell out and rolled across three lanes of speeding cars. Although every car was able to stop in time to avoid hitting the boy, no car was bumped by another. The mother screeched to a halt and ran to her small son only to discover that he was unhurt without a scratch or bruise on him! If you know anything about the freeways of Los Angeles, you, too, will consider this a miracle.

When the mother picked him up, he said, "Mommy, Mommy, did you see them?"

"See whom?" asked his mother.

"All the angels that stopped the cars!"

Elijah was afraid and ran for his life. When he came to Beersheba in Judah, he left his servant there, while he himself went a day's journey into the desert. He came to a broom tree, sat down under it and prayed that he might die. Then he lay down under the tree and fell asleep. All at once an angel touched him and said, "Get up and eat." He looked around, and there by his head was a cake of bread baked over hot coals, and a jar of water. He ate and drank and then lay down again. The angel of the LORD came back a second time and touched him and said, "Get up and eat, for the journey is too much for you" (I Kings 19:3-7).

FOOD FOR THOUGHT: Sometimes they come in disguise and you don't discover their true identity until the mystery is revealed. You never know when you come across an angel or when the circumstances of your life are such that you need a very special intervention. And, could it be that at times we ourselves can become the ministering angel for someone else at just the right moment?

"And he dreamed, and behold a ladder
set up on the earth, and the top of it reached to
heaven: and behold the angels of God
ascending and descending it."
—*Genesis 28:12*

Chapter 23

ANGELS IN THE BIBLE

The first biblically recorded appearance of angels was when two angels were set as guardians of the Garden of Eden. Their purpose was to keep the first man and woman from returning to the Garden and the Tree of Life, which was planted by God in the center of the Garden (Genesis 3:17, 22-24).

The last mention of angels was written by John in the final Revelation of Jesus Christ in the eternal New Jerusalem. This place is also known as heaven or the City of God, our future home where the River of Life flows and the Tree of Life is available for the healing of all who inhabit this heavenly home (Revelation 21:1-22:3).

Angels are created spiritual beings without earthly bodies, which is why they can appear in all kinds of human forms when they wish to be seen. Some are depicted as being full of light, and this appearance many times creates fear and awe in the humans who see them.

They have been granted awesome power, but are not to be worshiped because only God is one to be worshiped (Hebrews 1:1-14; Matthew 28:3-4; Psalm 104:4).

Angels can appear at your door, as testified to in many places in the Old Testament. Sometimes they appeared very ordinary. At times there was some difference, enough so that the people knew they were in the presence of an angel who had been sent from God. For example, Abraham invited three strangers to eat with him. In another place, an angel announced the birth of Samson to his parents, but it was only after they offered him a meal, which he refused and told them to burn it as a sacrifice. Then he left them, ascending to heaven in flames. We who live in the 21st century have been challenged to also show hospitality because there is the possibility of entertaining angels and not even knowing it (Genesis 18:1-14; Hebrews 13:2).

Angels frequently announced the birth of a special child, a child who would be important to the future of God's people. Most important was the angel who announced the coming of the most famous child ever born—Jesus! In fact, this was such an important task that we are given the name of the angel who was sent to bring the message—Gabriel. Gabriel was sent first to announce the birth of John the Baptist, and a few months later, returned to tell of the birth of the Christ child (Luke 1:5-38).

Angels who appear at the time of death to escort a dying person into the presence of God are told to us by

Jesus in the story of the rich man and Lazarus. What a wonderful, comforting possibility this is to the dying ones! This imagery is often used today and as you read more about the appearance of angels in our world, you will find many such instances (Luke 16:19-31).

Angels are seen as heavenly participants at the new birth of all who will inherit eternal salvation. They are shown as being concerned over what happens at the time of acceptance of the message of eternal life. They are depicted as rejoicing at each response to God's offer of love through salvation in Jesus Christ (Luke 15:3-10; I Thessalonians 4:16-17).

Angels participated with the life and ministry of Jesus Christ. They were present at His birth, His death, and His resurrection! They were present to help His parents escape the wrath of King Herod, at His baptism in the River Jordan, at His temptation in the wilderness, and as He agonized in the Garden of Gethsemane. They rolled away the stone from the door of His borrowed tomb, and they were there as He departed this world! (Matthew 2:13-14; 4:1-4; 28:1-2; Acts 1:3, 8-11)

And angels will be present at the judgment when they will pronounce it upon evil and be the ones to execute this judgment. The first incidence of this is when they told Abraham the fate of Sodom and Gomorrah. Jesus also told a number of parables relating to this judgment in which angels will have a part as they separate the wheat from the tares and more. John wrote in Revelations about how the angels will be present to pour out the final judgments on wickedness (Matthew 13:36-41; Revelation 8:2-12; 15:1).

Throughout all eternity, angels will participate in praise to God! Humans and angels are shown to be praising God in heaven. Together the redeemed of all ages and all peoples will be joined in eternity in praising God for His wonderful works and for the fact of our personal salvation! (Psalm 103:19-22; 148:1-2; Revelation 4:1-2; 5:11-12; 7:9-12)

"Every presence of an angel is a communication. Even when an angel crosses our path in silence, God has said to us, 'I am here. I am present in your life.'"
—*Tobias Palmer*

Chapter 24

THE FIRE FIGHTING ANGEL

As a young boy, Jimmy lived in a large old farm house located in rural North Dakota with his mother, father, and five younger brothers and sisters. Making a trip to town to get supplies or groceries would take all day. This incident occurred years before there was any electricity available to these rural farm people.

One day, Jimmy's parents had to go to another town on business and because of the distance they would have to stay overnight. Because Jimmy was the oldest, he was put in charge of the children. The younger ones were told that they must obey him because he was the head of the family in the absence of Mom and Dad.

The day went pretty well with Jimmy in charge. They all managed to do their assigned chores and had no major problems.

Some good natured wrestling and horse play was going on when Jimmy looked across the room at his three year old brother and watched to his horror that Benjamin was playing with a lighted candle. He was putting unlit matches into the flame and watching with great glee as they burst into flame. Before Jimmy could reach him, the candle tipped over and fire began to spread on the rug and the bedclothes.

No one could explain what happened next, but in the middle of the confusion and spreading fire, the children looked over at the bedroom door and saw a tall beautiful being standing in the doorway, which they later decided had to have been an angel. As they watched, the angel blew out the fire and turned and left. The children ran down the hall after the angel and downstairs and outside, but he had just disappeared.

Today, these brothers and sisters are all married and have children and grandchildren of their own, but when they have family get togethers during the holidays, sooner or later the conversation turns to the time they watched angel blow out the fire on a cold winter's night on a farm in norther North Dakota!

For he will command his angels concerning you to guard you in all your ways; they will lift you up in their hands, so that you will not strike your foot against a stone (Psalm 91:11-12).

FOOD FOR THOUGHT: God sends angels to His children to bring us protection under difficult circumstances. How often have you had angelic protect and didn't even know it was happening?

"Around our pillows
golden ladders will rise
and up and down the skies,
with winged sandals shod,
the angels come and go,
the Messengers of God!"
—*R.H. Stoddard*

Chapter 25

GOING HOME!

During a lifetime of ministry to people who were dying, I've discovered a few things about death. Many times I have been called to the hospital to be with someone who is dying. It takes about two or three minutes to know if I am dealing with Christians or not.

Death for a believer can be difficult and challenging, but it's not a time of despair because of the hope we have in the Lord.

I recall a young man in our church who, at the young age of 36, was dying of cancer. The disease had been discovered just a few short weeks previously and had quickly ravaged his body. I visited him and his wife and young son at home. On this occasion we were sitting together in the living room. He talked to his wife and son about going to heaven as if he were taking a short trip in the near future. I was so encouraged by him and yet almost overwhelmed as I listened with tears in my eyes.

He said to his young son, "And when I go to heaven this is what it will be like: First God will send His special angels and they will carry me home to heaven. When I get there I will miss you and Mommy, but just think about what Daddy's going to get to do! I will see Jesus, and be walking the streets of gold. I will listen to the angel choir sing their special songs and might even get to sing with them." He continued describing what heaven would be like and said that he would be waiting until his son also came to heaven where they would be a family forever. It was one of the most touching scenes I've ever witnessed!

Yes, believers die differently. The way that Christians face death is one of the strongest evidences of the reality of the Christian faith. So where do angels come into this picture? We have one very interesting story about this subject in Luke 16. It's the story about a rich man and a beggar and how they died. In this life, one was the beggar but in the next life he became the rich one and the rich man became the beggar asking for a drop of water.

The contrast at the moment of death is our point of interest. The rich man "died and was buried." Period. The next scene pictures him in hell. But when Lazarus died, it says that "the angels carried him to Abraham's side" (Luke 16:22). In his earthly life, the poor man's only consolation was that the dogs came and licked his sores, but at his death, angels were honored to carry him into heaven.

Going Home!

"Then I saw another angel flying in mid-air, and he had the eternal gospel to proclaim to those who live on the earth--to every nation, tribe, language and people" (Rev. 24:6).

FOOD FOR THOUGHT: In the book, *Somewhere Angels,* the author Larry Libby gives children this reason as to why angels will provide this special service to us at our time of death: "God wants you home so much He'll send His own angel to meet you. And don't be surprised if the angel is wearing a big smile!"

A SHINING HOPE

God grant that all who watch today
Beside their sepulchers of loss,
May find the great stone rolled away...
May see at last, with vision clear,
The shining angel standing near,
And through the dimly lighted soul
Again may joy's evangel roll
The glory of the Cross.
—*Julia H. Thayer*